MW01243715

Walking in Holiness

Savoy Mack

Thank You

To my Lord and Savior, Jesus Christ - thank you for entrusting me to write this life changing book. I pray that these words touch your people and bring them back to you.

To My Apostle, Dr. Onika Brown – thank you for pushing me to do this. I appreciate your encouragement and support. I never thought I would be an author but here I am.

To my family – thank you for your continued prayers and support. I love you all.

To everyone who will read this book – thank you for your support. I pray that the words in this book will cause you to press into the Holiness of God, and be changed by His power forever!

Blessings,
Elder Savoy Mack

WALKING IN HOLINESS

Table of Contents

WALKING IN HOLINESS

Introduction

The Holiness taught in the New Testament, and exemplified in the life of Christ, is the state in which the devil is defeated, and sin is shunned. It is the place where our will is in harmony with the will of God, where the Holy Spirit rules our lives in motive, affection, and action. It is the place where we may be beset by temptations but have the mastery over them. Holiness is Christ like sublimation of all our native human possibilities for good. Holiness is not so much an experience to be sought for itself, but rather is a by-product of a life fully consecrated to Christ. There can be no better definition for Holiness than this...*Holiness is Christlikeness*. In Christ we see the fruit of the spirit come to perfect fulfillment in our humanity. Jesus Christ is our highest definition and declaration of Holiness.

SAVOY MACK

Chapter 1: Define Holiness

Holiness is *the quality of being holy, set apart, and sanctified*. Holiness means *wholeness; to set a place apart for God to make is holy by the full development of the entire person-personality, virtue, and gifts*. The verb to consecrate **hagiazo** means *the offering of a sacrifice upon it*. The Christian has been dedicated and consecrated to God by the sacrifice of Jesus Christ.

The root idea of holiness is that of separation. The Jews were the holy people, the nation that was quite separate and different from other peoples. There is a link between holiness and spiritual power. The nineteenth century holiness movement, which started immediately after the Civil War, was a revival movement, and was almost exclusively Methodist in the beginning. Holiness has a collective communitarian character, which is revealed today in the manifest sons. We as the Bride of Christ cannot be but suspicious of any forms of holiness that has left unchanged a world filled with oppression, injustice, and exploitation.

3

If God is love and we are to be perfect and holy like our Father in Heaven, then it only follows that love and holiness entwine.

The restoration is here but much is yet to be perfected. When Jesus walked this earth, He was holy. You may say it was easy for him, He was born holy and without the original sin that we have inherited. That's true; however, the problem with us is that we often try too hard. Have you ever heard someone say to you that "no one said that the Christian life would be easy."? I have, many times. Jesus told us in Matthew 11:28 – "Come unto me, all ye that labor and heavy laden and I will give you rest. Take my yoke upon you, and learn of me, for I am meek and lowly in heart: and ye shall find rest unto my souls. Listen to me brethren for my yoke is easy, and my burden is light."

Chapter 2: Biblical Meaning of Holiness

In the Greek New Testament, the root hag is the basis of **hagiasmos**, translated "*holiness*", "*consecration*", "*sanctification,*" The hag words, translated by the Hebrew **qadosh**, literally mean, "*separate, contrasting with the profane.*" Thus, God, as holy, is separate in character from the things of the world. Things and people dedicated as holy to God and to His use are separate from the world and separate unto Him. Thus, "separation" is a major concept and a dynamic dimension of holiness. When God calls us to be holy, He is calling us to be separate from sin, separated unto Himself. We could also define holiness by its ramification, acknowledging that it is theologically valid, theoretically reasonable, philosophically our highest good, psychologically sound, ethically imperative, sociologically essential, biblically commanded, and experientially, a glorious possibility. These descriptions are all true but fall short of the most essential definition of holiness.

Chapter 3: Holiness of God

To say that the attribute of holiness is important is not to say that we understand it. Of all the attributes of God, in fact, this one is most misconstrued. The point is that the experience of confronting the Holy is supremely threading. The worshiper is drawn to the Holy, but at the same time he is terrified by it. The awe-inspiring, overpowering energy of the Holy threaten to destroy him.

Holiness of God
Exodus 15:11(NLT) – *"Who is like you among the gods, O LORD - glorious in holiness, awesome in splendor, performing great wonders?"*

God is consistently described as holy.

Habakkuk 1:11-12 (NLT) – *11 They sweep past like the wind and are gone. But they are deeply guilty, for their own strength is their god." 12 O Lord my God, my Holy One, you who are eternal—surely you do not plan to wipe us out? O Lord, our Rock, you have sent these Babylonians to correct us, to punish us for our many sins."*

God is holy cannot approve evil nor can he look on wickedness with favor. Holiness is the moral perfection (or excellence) of God's traits. It is His purity. Indeed, our shield belongs to the Lord, our King to the Holy One of Israel.

Isaiah 40:25 (NLT) - *"'To whom will you compare me? Who is my equal?' asks the Holy One."*

It is true that we must seek righteousness to be holy. That does not mean that we do it on our own; it means that we have made the decision to follow Christ and are willing to take upon His holy nature. This is the first step of faith, but it does not mean that we go to a preacher that says, recite after me, and then leave the church thinking that our decision for Christ is enough. To put on Jesus takes more than faith; faith is just the beginning. We deny our former way of thinking and begin thinking like Jesus. We love each other.

We do things differently than we used to. Our priorities have changed. Instead of ourselves being the center of the universe, we become God-centric. For those of you already making progress in this area, it is real in your life. He obviously deals with you in letting you know. He is there and you have a heart for him. Trust Him to lead you in the right direction.

Chapter 4: The Holy Spirit

It seems that with regards to the Holy Spirit, most of the emphasis is on what we can get from the spirit. While we certainly can gain a lot, and should know what that is, I want to first take time to learn about the nature and character of the Holy Spirit, and maybe just dwell on who the spirit is for a little while.

So, let's talk about the cool stuff the spirit provided.

- The Spirit was present at the formation of world

Genesis 1:2 (NLT) – *"The earth was formless and empty, and darkness covered the deep waters. And the Spirit of God was hovering over the surface of the waters."*

- The Spirit of God cannot be in strife with man.
- The Holy Spirit is not a vague, ethereal shadow, nor an impersonal force; He is a person equal in every way with God the Father and God the Son.

Matthew 28:19-20 (NLT) - [19] *"Therefore, go*

and make disciples of all the nations, baptizing them in the name of the Father and the Son and the Holy Spirit. **20** *Teach these new disciples to obey all the commands I have given you. And be sure of this: I am with you always, even to the end of the age." God is Father; Son is equally ascribed to the Holy Spirit."*

- When a person, becomes born again by believing and receiving Jesus Christ.

John 1:12-13 (NLT) *– **12** "But to all who believed him and accepted him, he gave the right to become children of God. **13** They are reborn—not with a physical birth resulting from human passion or plan, but a birth that comes from God."*

John 3: 3-21 (NLT) *– **3** "Jesus replied, "I tell you the truth, unless you are born again, you cannot see the Kingdom of God." **4** "What do you mean?" exclaimed Nicodemus. "How can an old man go back into his mother's womb and be born again?" **5** Jesus replied, "I assure you, no one can enter the Kingdom of God without being born of water and the Spirit. **6** Humans can reproduce only human life, but the Holy Spirit gives birth to spiritual life. **7** So don't be* surprised when I say, 'You must be born again.' 8 The wind blows wherever it wants. Just as you can hear the wind but can't tell where it comes from or where it is going, so you can't explain how people are born of the Spirit." 9 "How are these things possible?" Nicodemus asked. 10 Jesus replied, "You are a respected Jewish teacher, and yet you don't understand these things? 11 I assure you, we tell you what we know and have seen, and yet you won't believe our testimony. 12 But if you don't believe me when I tell you about earthly things, how can you possibly believe if I tell you about heavenly things? 13 No one has ever gone to heaven and returned. But the Son of Man has come down from heaven. 14 And as Moses lifted up the bronze snake on a pole in the wilderness, so the Son of Man must be lifted up, 15 so that everyone who believes in him will have eternal life. 16 "For this is how God loved the world: He gave his one and only Son, so that everyone who believes in him will not perish but have eternal life. 17 God sent his Son into the world not to judge the world, but to save the world through him. 18 "There is no judgment against anyone who believes in him. But anyone who does not believe in him has already been judged for not believing in God's one and only Son. 19 And *the judgment is based on this fact: God's light came into the world, but people loved the darkness more than the light, for their actions were evil. **20** All who do evil hate the light and refuse to go near it for fear their sins will be exposed. **21** But those who do what is right come to the light so others can see that they are doing what God wants."*

- God resides in that person through the Holy Spirit.

1 Cor 3:16 (NLT) – *" Don't you realize that all of you together are the temple of God and that the Spirit of God lives in you?"*

- The Holy Spirit has intellect.

1 Cor 2: 11 (NLT) – *"No one can know a person's thoughts except that person's own spirit, and no one can know God's thoughts except God's own Spirit."*

- The Holy Spirit has emotion.

Romans 15:30 (NLT) – *"Dear brothers and sisters, I urge you in the name of our Lord Jesus Christ to join in my struggle by praying to God for me. Do this because of your love for me, given to you by the Holy Spirit."*

- The Holy Spirit has a will.

1 Corinthians 12:11 (NLT) – *"It is the one*

and only Spirit who distributes all these gifts. He alone decides which gift each person should have."

- A primary role of the Holy Spirit is that He bears "witness" of Jesus Christ.

John 15:26 (NLT) - *"But I will send you the Advocate—the Spirit of truth. He will come to you from the Father and will testify all about me.*

- The Holy Spirit acts as a Christian's teacher.

2 Corinthians 2:9-14 (NLT) - *⁹"I wrote to you as I did to test you and see if you would fully comply with my instructions. ¹⁰ When you forgive this man, I forgive him, too. And when I forgive whatever needs to be forgiven, I do so with Christ's authority for your benefit, ¹¹ so that Satan will not outsmart us. For we are familiar with his evil schemes. ¹² When I came to the city of Troas to preach the Good News of Christ, the Lord opened a door of opportunity for me. ¹³ But I had no peace of mind because my dear brother Titus hadn't yet arrived with a report from you. So I said good-bye and went on to Macedonia to find him. ¹⁴ But thank God!*

He has made us his captives and continues to lead us along in Christ's triumphal procession. Now he uses us to spread the knowledge of Christ everywhere, like a sweet perfume.

- He reveals God's will and God's truth to a Christian.

John 16:13-14 (NLT) - *13 "When the Spirit of truth comes, he will guide you into all truth. He will not speak on his own but will tell you what he has heard. He will tell you about the future. 14 He will bring me glory by telling you whatever he receives from me."*

Chapter 5: Four Elements to Holiness

Majesty

Exodus 15:11 (NLT) - *"Who is like you among the gods, O Lord—glorious in holiness, awesome in splendor, performing great wonders?*

The elements of Majesty link's God's holiness to sovereignty, splendor, and grandeur.

Will

Exodus 20:4-5 (NLT) - *4 "You must not make for yourself an idol of any kind or an image of anything in the heavens or on the earth or in the sea. 5 You must not bow down to them or worship them, for I, the Lord your God, am a jealous God who will not tolerate your affection for any other gods. I lay the sins of the parents upon their children; the entire family is affected—even children in the third and fourth generations of those who reject me."*

God rejects every attack on his sole right as Lord of his creation, "You shall not make for yourself an idol in the form of anything in heaven above or on the earth beneath or in the waters below. You shall not bow down to them or worship them, for I, the Lord you God, am a jealous God, punishing the children for the sin of the Father to the third and fourth generation of those who hate me...

<u>Wrath</u>

Romans 1:18-19 (NLT) - **18** *"But God shows his anger from heaven against all sinful, wicked people who suppress the truth by their wickedness.* **19** *They know the truth about God because he has made it obvious to them."*

Wrath is the necessary and proper stance of Holy God to all who oppose him. He will not allow any person or thing to aspire to his place. Wrath to vindicate (clear, as from an accusation, justify) his name.

<u>Righteousness</u>

Revelation 15:3-4 (NLT) - **3** *"And they were singing the song of Moses, the servant of God, and the song of the Lamb: "Great and marvelous are your works, O Lord*

God, the Almighty. Just and true are your ways, O King of the nations. *4* Who will not fear you, Lord, and glorify your name? For you alone are holy. All nations will come and worship before you, for your righteous deeds have been revealed."

Whatever you do be righteous to God for he will do great things for you!!!

Chapter 6: Holiness is For You

Therefore, since we have a great high priest who has gone through the heavens, Jesus the Son of God, let us hold firmly to the faith we profess. For we do not have a high priest who is unable to sympathize with our weaknesses, but we have one who has been tempted in every way, just as we are-yet without sin," be perfect, before, as your heavenly Father is perfect.

1 Peter 1:14-16 (NLT) - [14] *"So you must live as God's obedient children. Don't slip back into your old ways of living to satisfy your own desires. You didn't know any better then.* [15] *But now you must be holy in everything you do, just as God who chose you is holy.* [16] *For the Scriptures say, "You must be holy because I am holy."*

Ephesians 5:1-2 (NLT) - *Imitate God, therefore, in everything you do, because you are his dear children.* **[2]** *Live a life filled with love, following the example of Christ. He loved us and offered himself as a sacrifice for us, a pleasing aroma to God.*

We are called to be holy in response to God's holiness as first seems to be all about an individual's relationship with God. Yet, that is only a small part of it. What we do, how we act, the things we say all affects other people. Consider this quote from the book *Come Away My Beloved* by Frances J. Roberts, "Eternal destinies are involved in the matters of thy holiness and thy faithfulness and thine obedience to my direction and will, but my love for thee is independent of these factors. Eternal destinies!"

I wrote another article that deals with how the things we do and say have far-reaching effects. It is called "Are you Building Up or Tearing Down"? The only way that people are going to see God in us is if we stand out from the crowd. We have to appear to be different than everyone else. How does that happen? We can't react in the expected way. We must be speaking words of edification when people expect to hear anger or some other negative emotion. We must love people who insist on being unlovable.

If we are constantly listening to what God wants us to be doing and saying, then we will be different than the rest. When we choose to do things, we are doing will not have an undertone of selfishness because the things we are doing will not be to serve our needs. We will look like everyone else, but we will shine with an unearthly light. We will shine with God's love, with truth, with strength, with peace, and with all the other things. God desires us to demonstrate. Other lives will be affected by what we say and do. Only God knows what the long-term effects will be. We just have to trust him to know and then obey.

Chapter 7: The Grace of Holiness

Throughout the history of Christendom, there has been a constant struggle to strike a balance in this one area. Satan has had a field day at every turn. The issue is holiness, and both the definition of it and performance of it have been characterized by a pendulum that swings from one extreme to another. On the other hand, we are called one by God to be separate and distinct and different. We are "holy" ones, not contaminated by the sin in the world nor drawn to it.

On the other hand, we were sent into the world to be lights, and as such we are to infiltrate a sinful. Lost and dying world by penetrating the darkness. Jesus, our example of perfect holiness, spent time with publicans and sinners, and unlike the Scribes and Pharisees. He touched lepers and blind men and ate with the like of tax collectors and thieves. He was accused by the religious hierarchy of fellowshipping with the wrong crowd, and thus was considered "unholy". He healed on the Sabbath, and forgave prostitutes and murders of their sins,

Holy? To them, He didn't understand or grasp the meaning of the word. To them, holy meant uncontaminated.

For that wounded man by the side of the road, it meant don't touch him or you be unclean. Grace, then, is the answer. We are drawn near unto us. We are to resist the devil, and he will flee from us. It is to be a constant, consistent process. We must not be satisfied that we are not losing ground, either. We are to be growing, in ever-increasing splendor, from one degree of glory to another. That means that there a year ago. With every passing hour, Jesus ought to be more real to us and dearer to us.

Chapter 8: Scripture Mentions Holiness and Holy

2 Corinthians 7:1 NLT - "Because we have these promises, dear friends, let us cleanse ourselves from everything that can defile our body or spirit. And let us work toward complete holiness because we fear God."

1 Peter 1:15-16 (NLT) - [15] But now you must be holy in everything you do, just as God who chose you is holy. [16] For the Scriptures say, "You must be holy because I am holy."

John 15:4 (NLT) - Remain in me, and I will remain in you. For a branch cannot produce fruit if it is severed from the vine, and you cannot be fruitful unless you remain in me.

John 5:14 (NLT) - But afterward Jesus found him in the Temple and told him, "Now you are well; so stop sinning, or something even worse may happen to you."

John 8:11 (NLT) - "No, Lord," she said. And Jesus said, "Neither do I. Go and sin no more."

Matthew 5:8 (NLT) – "God blesses those whose hearts are pure, for they will see God."

Romans 12:2 (NLT) – "Don't copy the behavior and customs of this world, but let God transform you into a new person by changing the way you think. Then you will learn to know God's will for you, which is good and pleasing and perfect."

Philippians 3:15 (NLT) – "Let all who are spiritually mature agree on these things. If you disagree on some point, I believe God will make it plain to you."

Ephesians 1:4 (NLT) – "Even before he made the world, God loved us and chose us in Christ to be holy and without fault in his eyes."

Ephesians 5:27 (NLT) – "He did this to present her to himself as a glorious church without a spot or wrinkle or any other blemish. Instead, she will be holy and without fault."

Endnotes

Acts 1: 4-8 (NLT) - [4] Once when he was eating with them, he commanded them, "Do not leave Jerusalem until the Father sends you the gift he promised, as I told you before. [5] John baptized with[b] water, but in just a few days you will be baptized with the Holy Spirit." [6] So when the apostles were with Jesus, they kept asking him, "Lord, has the time come for you to free Israel and restore our kingdom?" [7] He replied, "The Father alone has the authority to set those dates and times, and they are not for you to know. [8] But you will receive power when the Holy Spirit comes upon you. And you will be my witnesscs, telling people about me everywhere—in Jerusalem, throughout Judea, in Samaria, and to the ends of the earth."

1 Corinthians 1:30 (NLT) - [30] "God has united you with Christ Jesus. For our benefit God made him to be wisdom itself. Christ made us right with God; he made us pure and holy, and he freed us from sin."

Ephesians 5:25-27 (NLT) - ²⁵ *"For husbands, this means love your wives, just as Christ loved the church. He gave up his life for her ²⁶ to make her holy and clean, washed by the cleansing of God's word. ²⁷ He did this to present her to himself as a glorious church without a spot or wrinkle or any other blemish. Instead, she will be holy and without fault."*

Hebrews 3:4 (NLT) – *"For every house has a builder, but the one who built everything is God."*

Hebrews 6: 1-3 (NLT) – ¹ *"So let us stop going over the basic teachings about Christ again and again. Let us go on instead and become mature in our understanding. Surely we don't need to start again with the fundamental importance of repenting from evil deeds and placing our faith in God. ² You don't need further instruction about baptisms, the laying on of hands, the resurrection of the dead, and eternal judgment. ³ And so, God willing, we will move forward to further understanding."*

1 John 3:6 (NLT) – *"Anyone who*

continues to live in him will not sin. But anyone who keeps on sinning does not know him or understand who he is."

John 20:21-23 (NLT) - 21 "Again he said, "Peace be with you. As the Father has sent me, so I am sending you." 22 Then he breathed on them and said, "Receive the Holy Spirit. 23 If you forgive anyone's sins, they are forgiven. If you do not forgive them, they are not forgiven."

Romans 5:12-16 (NLT) – 12 "When Adam sinned, sin entered the world. Adam's sin brought death, so death spread to everyone, for everyone sinned. 13 Yes, people sinned even before the law was given. But it was not counted as sin because there was not yet any law to break. 14 Still, everyone died—from the time of Adam to the time of Moses— even those who did not disobey an explicit commandment of God, as Adam did. Now Adam is a symbol, a representation of Christ, who was yet to come. 15 But there is a great difference between Adam's sin and God's gracious gift. For the sin of this one man, Adam, brought death to many. But even *greater is God's wonderful grace and his gift of forgiveness to many through this other man, Jesus Christ. ¹⁶ And the result of God's gracious gift is very different from the result of that one man's sin. For Adam's sin led to condemnation, but God's free gift leads to our being made right with God, even though we are guilty of many sins."*